Beauty of
Illinois

Beauty of
Illinois

Text: Andrea Kennett
Concept & Design: Robert D. Shangle

First Printing October, 1990
Published by LTA Publishing Company
2735 S.E. Raymond Street, Portland, Oregon 97202
Robert D. Shangle, Publisher

"Learn about America in a beautiful way."

Library of Congress Cataloging-in-Publication Data

Kennett, Andrea.
   Beauty of Illinois.
     .1. Illinois — Description and travel — 1981 — Views.
I. Title.
F542.K46   1989   977.3   89-12525
ISBN 0-917630-79-3
ISBN 0-917630-78-4 (pbk.)

Copyright © 1990 by LTA Publishing Company
Printed in United States of America

Contents

Introduction	7
Land of Lincoln	8
North Central	12
Chicago	15
Great River Trail	68
Little Egypt	76

Introduction

"The heartland of our country" and "the true America" are expressions oftentimes used to describe Illinois. Its identity, with the rural lowland that comprises most of the state, contrasts sharply with the major cities of America. French-Canadian explorer Louis Joliet, who trekked through the Illinois plains in 1673 with Jesuit priest Father Jacques Marquette, summed it up by saying, "No better soil can be found . . . [it is] the most beautiful and most easily settled [land]."

Bounded by five states and Lake Michigan, this north central state marks the locale where East meets West. Known as a Mid-western state, Illinois offers an unbounded variety of weather due to its geographic location.

So strategically located, Illinois has been called a "crossroads state." Major transportation arteries — air, land, and water travel — all intersect in Illinois, providing economic status.

Illinois derives its name from a French adaptation of the Illini Indians, who formed a North American confederation of tribes residing in the area before the white man arrived. They called themselves "Illiniwek," or "full grown man," or as suggested by missionary Father Louis Hennepin, "complete and perfect man." Demoralized by disease, famine, and war, the last of the Illiniwek left the state in 1833 to resettle in Kansas. But they left a permanent mark on the state.

This book pays tribute to the scenic beauty of Illinois: the rolling green and russet prairies; the massive woodlands and craggy rocks; the quiet and exciting beauty of the waterways. Join our wanderings through the great prairie state — Illinois.

— A.K.

Land of Lincoln

Early explorers were enthused about the lush grasslands and fertile soil that composes most of Illinois. Ninety percent of the state is contained in the Till Plains.

The first settlers found almost half of the state wooded, with great prairies stretching between creeks and other waters, and the surface of the land strewn with wild flowers and thick man-high grass. The treeless land earned Illinois the nickname of Prairie State. The timber industry and agriculture has chopped away much of the forest and grassland and replaced it with the checkerboard pattern of farmland. Illinois is a part of the Corn Belt that extends westward from Ohio to Kansas and Nebraska, and is often referred to as the "garden spot" and "breadbasket" of the nation. Illinois is also known for her people. Abraham Lincoln is her most famous citizen. In honor of the 16th president, Illinois is called the "Land of Lincoln."

Since 1830, when the tall, gangly Kentuckian came to Illinois, the nation was destined to experience some of its most dramatic moments. The Civil War President's life is tightly woven into the history of Illinois. Nearly every town and village claims some association with the Great Emancipator. Most of these boasts are truly genuine, since Lincoln's judicial circuit-riding days covered 11,000 square miles, providing contact with many communities. The Lincoln Heritage Trail traces 1,000 miles of his route, from Kentucky and Indiana into Illinois, entering the prairie land south of Danville.

The heart of the Lincoln story begins and ends in Springfield. Here, Lincoln married Mary Todd and practiced law for 20 years, with the exception of a two-year term he served in Congress from 1847-49, and during his years as President. Lincoln is buried in Springfield's Park Ridge cemetery, on the north side of the city. The spire of the tomb rises 117 feet above an elevated base inscribed with reliefs of Lincoln's contributions to the country. It serves as a reminder to visitors that the man, in his words and by his actions, "belongs to the ages," as written in the epitaph by his Secretary of War, Edwin M. Stanton.

The Lincoln Historic District features the two-story frame house, known as the Nenian Edwards home, where the Lincolns were married and first lived.

The area surrounding Springfield is the country where Lincoln grew to adulthood. Six years of his early adult life were spent in New Salem, about 60 miles west of Springfield on the Sagamon River. Here he was store clerk, steamboat pilot, postmaster, and finally, law student. Much of the town has been rebuilt to recall the Lincoln period; only the Onstod Cooper Shop is an original structure.

The circuit trail out of Springfield, which Lincoln created during his law days, left indelible marks on the communities he visited. As the story goes, the people of Mount Pulaska, to the north, gave him his nickname of "Honest Abe." The Postville citizens renamed their village, in 1853, Lincoln — the only town named after the man while he was still alive. Annually, the town of Lincoln observes the National Railsplitting Festival to recall its namesake. As a lawyer Lincoln traveled as far north as Ottawa, which later saw the first Lincoln-Douglas debate in the town's Washington Park. Decatur, east of Springfield, dominates the Lincoln story. He made his first political speech here in 1830, at the age of 21.

Just east of town, along the Sagamon river, is the restored family home of Lincoln and his parents, who first settled in Illinois in 1830. Thomas and Sarah Lincoln resettled their family seven miles south of Charleston, located in Coles County, about 80 miles southeast of Springfield. This was their final home. Lincoln's parents are buried in nearby Shiloh Cemetery a few miles west of Charleston.

The area outside of Charleston offers an abundance of adventures for today's participants. The Embarras River (pronounced "embarrah") found in Fox Ridge State Park and Lake Shelbyville, attract boaters, anglers, and hikers.

In nearby Arthur and Arcola, the Amish were settling, and, today, they still lead that uncomplicated life of the mid-1800s.

Lincoln's legal skill was felt as far west as Beardstown, where, in 1858, he successfully defended the alleged murderer, Duff Armstrong, in the famous Almanac Murder Trial.

Words of another sort represent the territory north of Beardstown. Edgar Lee Masters made famous the Spoon River Valley, from Lewistown to London Mills, in his *Spoon River Anthology*. His couplets began in Lewistown's Oak Hill Cemetery as epitaphs for his friends and neighbors.

Another poet, Carl Sandburg, was born in Galesburg. Between Galesburg and Beardstown, on 162 acres at Dickson Mounds Museum near Havana, are some of Illinois' finest archeological displays, tracing the state's pre-history.

The Shaker influence came to Illinois at Bishop Hill, north of Galesburg, near Kewanee. Thanks to the restoration efforts, remnants of this prairie utopia have remained. Swedish Janssonites followed Eric Jansson to form a colony of highly skilled farmers and craftsmen. The community thrived until 1850, when Jansson was killed by a man who sought to free his wife from the colony. The pristine white Colony Church was the first permanent structure at Bishop Hill and was the first restored. Bishop Hill was the favorite subject of the primitive-style painter Olof Krans, a resident of the community.

Peoria dominates the Illinois River Valley. The central river town is renowned for its luxurious old mansions, notably the 14-room, pre-Civil War Flanagan House and the elegant Victorian-style Morran House. In 1680 the Italian mercenary, Henri de Tonti, and the Sieur de La Salle, built the first French fort in the West near Peoria. The fort was built during the harsh winter and was aptly named Fort Creve Coeur, or Fort Heartbreak.

Sheffield's St. Peter's Church, nearby, is the nation's largest Danish Lutheran congregation. The Queen of Denmark, Margarethe II, rededicated the 19th-century church in 1976.

Wildlife Prairie Park, west of Peoria, between Routes 116 and 8, uses a special habitat setting that allows the animals native to Illinois to be viewed in a natural area, free of a barred enclosure.

Industrial and commercial centers of Champaign and Urbana, and Kankakee, farther north, break up the farmland in the eastern portion of the central prairie.

North Central

An ordinance, in 1787, claimed for Wisconsin the land from the coast of Lake Michigan, the site of Chicago, the northern terminus of the Illinois River and Michigan Canal to the lead mines of Galena. Illinois officially claimed the land when Nathanial Pope, a delegate to Congress, presented the statehood petition in 1818 and included the area.

North-central Illinois is a vague classification for the region buffering Wisconsin and the central prairie — basically the area north of Interstate Highway 80. The hilly, restive, driftless region on the northwest contrasts with the spectacular sandstone formation, woodlands, and farmlands of the central valley. Then there is the bustling commercial hub of Chicago along the Lake Michigan shore.

Rockford, northernmost city and seat of Winnebago County, is the second largest city in the state. This machinery-manufacturing center provides a focal point for the north-central region.

The Sauk Indian Chief, Black Hawk, was born in 1767 in Rockford, then called Saukenuk, and resided in this prominent Sauk village until 1829. Black Hawk figured prominently in the Indian struggle to protect their lands against the white man's encroachment.

The drive from Rockford, along the Rock River to the Quad Cities, is known as the Black Hawk Trail. From the Mississippi banks in the Quad Cities, the Sauk Indian chief admonished white settlers, saying, "The Rock River was a beautiful country. . . . It is now yours. Keep it as we did." Black Hawk State Park, at the south edge of Rock Island, commemorates his words and hosts an Indian pow-wow each Labor Day.

Freeport, 29 miles west of Rockford, is known chiefly as the location of the second Lincoln-Douglas Debate held August 27, 1858.

From the Rock River's birth, near South Beloit in the north, the river follows a pre-glacial channel. Geologists believe that the river once joined the Illinois near Hennepin, before glaciers diverted its stream to meet the Mississippi at Moline.

Southwest along the Rock River on State Highway 2 stands a 48-foot statue of the Chief Black Hawk, high above the river's east bank. The statue, by Loredo Taft, commemorates Black Hawk's love of the grove of virgin pine, flowers, and wildlife of the area that is now Lowden State Park. Another Taft sculpture, the Soldier's Monument, stands in the courthouse square in Oregon, Illinois.

People still hike the Chicago-Iowa pioneer trail to view the mossy cliffs and contoured hills of hickory, basswood, and the southernmost stand of white pines in the Midwest, at White Pine Forest State Park, west of the town of Oregon.

Thirty miles southwest of Oregon, in lower Whiteside County, is Prophetstown, which derived its name from the ill-fated return of Black Hawk's Sauk Indians. They came to Prophetstown on the advice of Winnebago, prophet Wablkieshiek (White Cloud), when spring crops failed in Iowa. The unauthorized crossing brought troops into Stillman Valley, farther north near Byron, where tension provoked gunfire and began a 15-month Indian battle. A 50-foot granite shaft in Stillman Valley pays homage to the dead of the first engagement of the Black Hawk War.

Father Jacques Marquette held the first Christian service in Illinois in 1675, on the west bank of the Illinois River near Starved Rock State Park. He also built the Mission of the Immaculate Conception, which was followed by a string of now-vanished French forts. The most important fort was one built in 1682 by Robert Cavalier, known as Sieur de La Salle. The fort was named Fort St. Louis, to honor the king of France.

The east bank of the river, southwest of Peoria, has a colorful history brought about by the horror stories of the "Iron Hand." The fearful Indians gave Henri Tonti this name because of the metal hook that replaced his amputated hand. Tonti built Fort Creve Coeur a year after Fort St. Louis was abandoned.

Illinois' only unspoiled sand dunes, found in the Lake Michigan Beach area north of Chicago, have attracted a strange mix of people to Illinois State Park. First explored by 17th-century trappers and missionaries, the park served as the filming site of the first American western in 1914. A little farther west, the state's largest single concentration of lakes, the Chain O'Lakes, attracts anglers for an annual fishing derby. The 4,000-acre park borders three of the ten lakes in the Fox Chain and is located on U.S. Highway 12, about 40 miles northwest of Chicago. Another popular retreat from Chicago's urban life is found at Rock Cut State Park near Caledonia, a land-grant park established in 1847 by Zachary Taylor.

Chicago

Few toddling towns have matured to demand such national prominence as has Chicago. Culture, finance, art and science, education, and entertainment combine in the "Queen City of the Lakes." Positioned in the northeastern corner of Illinois, Chicago claims much of the Great Lake Plains and Illinois lakeshore.

The central location of Illinois and its rich resources helped make Chicago the transportation center of this nation. O'Hare International Airport handles air traffic for approximately 2,100 planes daily. It is one of the busiest airports in the world. Most of the railroads in Illinois have terminals in Chicago. Passenger vehicles and commercial trucks on transcontinental routes go in or near Chicago.

Chicago, the leading port in the Great Lakes, is one of the nation's busiest water ports. The Great Lakes link Chicago with the states east of Illinois via the St. Lawrence Seaway. Chicago is the only inland city with combined river, lake, and ocean traffic.

Mention Chicago in other parts of the country, and many people envision Al Capone, Elliott Ness, Bugs Moran, and the St. Valentine's Day Massacre of 1929; the stockyards and grain elevators. Those claims to fame are gone. The stockyards that Carl Sandburg said typified Chicago as "hog butcher to the world," have moved to Joliet, replaced in Chicago by an industrial complex.

Joliet and Marquette were the first Europeans known to visit the site of Chicago in 1673. A Black explorer and fur trader, Jean Baptist Point du Sable, built the first permanent cabin in 1779. Fort Dearborn, a blockhouse and stockade, was constructd in 1804, but fell to an Indian massacre in 1812. What remained developed into Chicago, laid out in a square-grid pattern that survives today. The village's name was derived from the Algonquin word *"checagou*, meaning "wild garlic," "skunks," or "skunk run," depending upon which translation one accepts. Pioneers shaped Chicago into a railroad hub and commercial industrial center by 1850.

In 1860 Chicago was the site of an event to alter the future of the Union Republicans gathered in the Wigwam, a large wooden building, and after a series of raucous sessions, chose Abraham Lincoln as the party's presidential candidate. The Wigwam, at what is now Lake Street and Wacker Drive, is now a part of history.

The consistency of Chicago as a political center has earned it the jibe Windy City, in reference to hot air generated by political events. True, there are gusts of wind that come off Lake Michigan, but they are rarely the gales of popular stereotype.

Modern architecture was born in Chicago, which continues as a foundation for innovative design. Pioneers Frank Lloyd Wright, Ludwig Mies van der Roche, Louis Sullivan, Daniel Burnham, and John Root left major imprints on the skyline. Burnham fathered the maximum-use plan of the lakefront to beautify the city. After Mrs. O'Leary's cow kicked over a lantern, igniting hay in the DeKoven Street barn and burning one-third of the city in the Great Fire of 1871, the Chicago School of Architecture led a renaissance in 1883 to rebuild a beautiful city.

Giant buildings stretch upward throughout the city, reinforcing Chicago's fame as birthplace of the skyscraper. Now Chicago claims ownership to three of the world's tallest buildings: the Sears Tower — 110 stories, (1,468$\frac{1}{2}$ feet); the Standard Oil Building — 80 stories, (1,135 feet); the 100 story John Hancock Center — "Big John" at 1,125 feet high. Its exterior X-trusses give it a unique appearance. A spectacular view of the city is afforded from "Big John's" top-floor observation windows. Just south of "Big John" stands the Chicago Water Tower, surviving landmark of the Great Fire, and now home of the Visitor Information Center.

State Capitol Building, Springfield

Lincoln's New Salem Historic Site

Springfield Lake, Springfield

Thomas Rees Carillon, Springfield

Covered Bridge near Springfield

Near Amboy

Southern Illinois Farmland

Chicago and Grant Park

Grant Park, Chicago

Lincoln's Home National Historic Site

Along Lake Michigan at Evanston

Illinois River near Ottawa

Moon Rising in Jo Daviess County

Illinois Beach State Park

Adler Planetarium, Chicago

Mary's River Covered Bridge, Near Chester

Chicago

Near Dixon, Illinois

Rock River, Kankakee River State Park

Grist Mill New Salem Historic Site

Southern Illinois Farmland

Near Stockton, Illinois

Mississippi River Sunset near Nauvoo

Near Chester, Illinois

Garden of the Gods area, Shawnee National Forest

New Salem National Historic Site

Sunset on a farm near Casey, Illinois

Mississippi River near Savanna

Nauvoo, Illinois

Buckingham Fountain and Rose Garden in Grant Park, Chicago

Northwestern University Campus, Evanston

Evanston Lighthouse

Conservatory in Lincoln Park, Chicago

Soldiers Field and Burnham Yacht Club, Chicago

Lincoln Park, Chicago

Northwest Illinois Farmland

Lincoln's Log Cabin near Campbell, Illinois

The Old State Capitol Building, Springfield

Starved Rock State Park

Crab Orchard, Illinois

Lincoln's Tomb, Springfield

Thomson Hill Covered Bridge near Cowden

State Capitol Grounds, Springfield

Chicago

Near Pulleys Mill, Illinois

Shawnee National Forest

Near Casey, Illinois

Kankakee River

The Old Water Tower begins the Magnificent Mile, a name given Michigan Avenue's river-to-lake stretch of exclusive business offices. Across Michigan Avenue is Water Tower Place, royalty of the mile, with several glass elevators in a seven-level atrium mall.

Old Town, a quick detour west of Michigan Avenue, combines an old ethnic community with bohemian boutiques. The architecture and frequent stained-glass windows reflect the ancestry of the former German settlement. The area thrived after the Great Fire, but by the mid-20th century, it had deteriorated. New interest in the 1950s revived the area as businesses moved in and homes were renovated. Recently, Old Town changed into the "Greenwich Village of the Midwest."

Fort Dearborn, Chicago's first settlement, is marked by bronze tablets recording the city's history. Mosaic walls and Tiffany windows create a splendid architectural beauty at the neighboring Chicago Public Library Cultural Center. Another cultural landmark, the Chicago Art Institute, stands majestically farther south on Michigan Avenue, where bronze lions guard one of the world's foremost galleries of French Impressionist art, representing every major artist. More modern tastes are satisfied at the unique Museum of Contemporary Art. Classical music is presented across from the Chicago Art Institute in Orchestra Hall, home of the top-rated Chicago Symphony Orchestra.

Architectural tours of Chicago's famous Loop aptly begin at the ArchiCenter, where continuous exhibits display the city's contributions to architecture. Tours are also offered by the Chicago Architecture Foundation from the historic Glessner House on Prairie Avenue.

The Loop is defined by Chicago's encircling rapid transit system, bounded by Wabash Avenue on the east, Wells on the west, and Van Buren and Lake streets on the south and north. A prominent part of the Loop is State Street, "that Great Street," now rivaled by Michigan Avenue as the street for shopping. State Street has been transformed into an expensive shopping plaza open only to pedestrian traffic.

South and east of the Loop is the Field Museum of Natural History and the Museum of Science and Industry, built as the Palace of Fine Arts for the World's Columbian Exposition of 1893.

Unique architecture shares space with innovative art at the Federal Center at Adams and Dearborn. The Monadnock Building, off Dearborn Street, reigned as the world's tallest office building with 16 stories, when erected in 1891. It remains the largest building constructed with masonry walls.

Chicago's financial district bows only to New York's in size. The Midwest's Wall Street thrives with the Chicago Board of Trade, the world's largest grain exchange. Nearby, the Chicago Mercantile Exchange and the Midwest Stock Exchange can be found. On the north bank of the river, on Wells, stands the Merchandise Mart, world's largest commercial buyer center, boasting 97 acres of floor space. Its neighbor, the Apparel Center, showcases top fashion designers.

At one time Chicago was the ethnic center of the Midwest. A German settlement still centers around Lincoln and Lawrence. A Polish area spreads out from the boutiques in the 1200 blocks of Milwaukee Avenue. A Lithuanian area is near 40th and South Archer streets. Chinatown, along Wentworth Avenue south of Cermak Road, is a picturesque area of shops and restaurants. The suburb of Highland Park is largely an Italian community.

Considering the city's fame for concrete and steel creations, it is surprising to realize the city is 19-percent park and playground and has another 6,000 acres of federal lands providing verdant buffers of woodland along the waterways and suburbs. Boating and fishing are popular. Lists of fishing areas and boat ramps are available through the Forest Preserve District and the Chicago Park District Divison.

Lincoln Park, along Lake Shore Drive from North to Hollywood avenues, is the largest city park. Along with its monuments, beaches, playgrounds, and a bird sanctuary, Lincoln Park is home of the 312-acre Lincoln Park Conservatory. Lincoln Park Zoo is set in 30 city blocks of beach.

Lake Michigan once covered the site of Grant Park, between Randolph and McFetridge streets. Expansion desires led the Illinois Central Railroad to fill in the area to allow for the extension of its tracks to the Chicago River. A rose garden and formal gardens provide a magnificent setting for concerts featured in the band shell.

Burnham Park, connecting Grant and Jackson parks, was the site of the Century of Progress World's Fair in 1932-33. It boasts of more than 5,000 species of flora. Soldier Field sports stadium is a memorial to Chicagoans who died in World War I. Jackson Park on the south was the scene of the Columbian Exposition of 1893. Garfield Park Conservatory, on the park's north end, is considered the world's largest conservatory housed under one roof.

The abandoned Illinois-Michigan Canal, which, in 1849, connected Chicago's port to western waterways, now provides one of Illinois' major recreation areas with 15 miles of parkway. A museum in Lockport contains exhibits that tell the history of the canal. Originally, the Chicago River emptied into Lake Michigan, but engineers reversed the river's flow with the installation of the canal, to keep sewage from polluting the lake. A city sewer system was installed, but swampy soil precluded burying sewer lines. Instead, streets were raised to cover the pipes, blocking front entrances to many homes. Consequently, residents built steps to the second floors. Homes built before the turn of the century still have the front door in the second story.

Opened in 1933, the Illinois Waterway replaced the outdated canal. The 327-mile toll-free barge route connects Lake Michigan at Chicago and the Mississippi River at Grafton, following a route proposed in the 17th century by Joliet and the Sieur de La Salle.

Great River Trail

The Mississippi River is revered by the men who inhabit the banks, their lives revolving around the waters. A few years ago, all of the states through which the Mississippi flows organized and gave a name, the Great River Trail, to the 1,750 miles of road and highway that most closely parallel the river. The "road" enters Illinois by way of Wisconsin where, at the confluence of the Wisconsin and Mississippi rivers, Marquette and Joliet discovered the "Father of Waters" 300 years ago. The Great River Trail winds 510 miles down along western Illinois, in and out of Iowa, as often out of sight of the river as in sight.

From its northern debut in Illinois at East Dubuque in the rugged Driftless Area, the Mississippi forms the full western border of the state, carving white limestone cliffs before meeting the Rock River in the industrial Quad cities. Its path continues west and south to Nauvoo, whose present serenity belies a turbulent past. It then bends eastward to another industrial complex at East St. Louis before ending its trek in the prairie state at the Cairo waterfront.

Driftless Area

Glaciers, which gouged smooth most of Illinois, spared the northwest corner, leaving the area rough with the state's tallest hills and deepest valleys. Jo Davies County composes much of this region, called the Driftless Area in reflection of the untamed terrain. Rivers flow free in the same beds they carved a half-million years ago before the glaciers.

One of the state's most scenic areas, Apple River Canyon State Park, lies off State Highway 78 in the northeastern edge of the region. The tiny Apple River has gently eroded a twisting bed through limestone, carving colorful rock formations, bluffs, and ravines. Charles Mound, the highest elevation in the prairie state at 1,241 feet, contains many secrets of prehistoric man on this continent.

The Mississippi River enters Illinois in the Dubuque Hills and continues toward the prairie. Just south of the Wisconsin border, along a bend in the river, stands Galena, a town that time has forgotten, and one of the prettiest communities in Illinois. Once a bustling city, zinc and lead deposits promised Galena a seemingly limitless future. Now the town counts a population of about 3,800, far reduced from an 1860 census of 15,000. Much of the town was built on the bluffs, overlooking the mines and the river. Most of the period buildings are still in use, including the Old Custom House of classical design, the Old de Soto House where Lincoln spoke, and the Old Market House at Market Square. Built in 1845, it is the oldest remaining market in the Midwest. The Market House served as the city hall until 1936.

Two houses claim ties to Ulysses S. Grant. A humble house was his residence, when Grant lived briefly in Galena, tending his father's harness and leather store. After his victorious return from the Civil War, grateful residents gave him a two-story brick house, now restored as a state memorial.

The unique past of Galena survives modernization, instituted through the many unusual names that title parts of the town. For example, Shakerag Street recalls the times when women stood on the bluff-front porches and shook cleaning dusters to call their men home from the lead mines for their meals.

The drive from Galena on U.S. Highway 20 to Freeport covers some of the prettiest 40 miles in the state. Sparsely populated, the region includes small, colorful communities such as Elizabeth, a one-time lead-mining community now popular for its general stores.

Mississippi Palisades State Park, southeast of Galena and two miles north of Savannah, combines a visual contrast of 250-foot cliffs, dark marshes, and open meadows. The park is famous for its bluff-top views of the river: Sunset Trail provides hikers their best views.

Mid-River

A good place to begin an exploration of the Great River Trail's journey through the prairie is at Fulton, just south of the Driftless Area, named for Robert Fulton, whose invention of the steamboat harnessed the mighty Mississippi waters for modern commerce. State Highway 84 claims the honor as the Great River Trail in northern Illinois.

Morrison Rockwood State Park provides a wildlife sanctuary and serenity for humans, a few miles east on U.S. Highway 30. From Fulton the Mississippi makes two big bends before tumbling into the Quad Cities commercial/industrial complex (Rock Island and Moline, Illinois, and Davenport and Bettendorf, Iowa). Rock Island served as a Civil War ordnance depot and prisoner-of-war camp; a Confederate cemetery remains. Now Arsenal Island houses Rock Island Arsenal, the largest manufacturing arsenal in the country. Of visitor interest are the John M. Browning Memorial Museum of guns, the Clock Tower Building, and Fort Armstrong's blockhouse replica.

Moline claims the distinction of "Farm Implement Capital of America," as center of the John Deere organization. Deere, in 1837, invented the self-scouring steel plow in Grant Detour, in the north-central area. His plow enabled farmers to till land where prairie grass grew higher than man and horse, and the roots grew deeper into the soil than a wood plow could handle.

Two religious movements marked the decades before the 20th century, both in the same river town. In the 1820s the Indians sold the site of Nauvoo for two sacks of corn. The community grew into the most vibrant, successful river town, and by the 1840s it grew into the largest city in Illinois, with a population swelling over 27,000.

Joseph Smith and 15,000 Mormon followers from Missouri founded Nauvoo as the church's capital in 1839. The state general assembly granted the Mormons immunity from outside interference, political freedom, and free religious practices. But deep-seated antagonisms and prejudice against Mormonism in the nearby countryside erupted into violence. Smith and his brother, Hyrum, were killed by a lynch mob in 1844, when they were taken into "protective custody" at Carthage Jail. The jail stands restored as an historic reminder of the hateful incidents in Carthage, located inland about 40 miles in central Hancock County.

Brigham Young led the Mormon community to Salt Lake City, Utah, two years later. The Utah Mormons and the Reorganized Church of Jesus Christ of Latter-day Saints in Missouri are today restoring the community of Nauvoo to retell their story.

After the Mormons left, Nauvoo shrunk into a ghost town. In 1849 Etienne Cabet, a French lawyer and politician, established a utopian community there for the French and German settlers, who were known as Icarians. The settlements withered away, but the orchards and vineyards the Icarians planted flourished, supporting a winery industry today. The grape harvest in September is celebrated every Labor Day weekend with the picturesque Wedding of the Wines and Cheese Ceremony.

Downriver, Quincy typifies a more sedate way of life, where a pillared, 17-room southern mansion, located on the river front, houses the County Historical Museum. An aerial cablecar takes passengers up the bluffs to Quinsippi Island Recreation Area.

Siloam Springs State Park, east on State Highway 104, once was believed to be a magical source for medical water, a story given credence by a 102-year-old war veteran who credited the local springs for his longevity. The 3,000 acres of parkland spills from the east edge of Adams County into Brown County.

Prehistoric Indians are documented as residing in Green County, about 70 miles north of St. Louis, from the famous archeological dig on the Theodore Koster farm. Sheltered by bluffs, the farm contains a dozen district horizons of prehistoric communities dating to 6,000 B.C., long before the construction of Stonehenge in England or the great Egyptian pyramids. Scientific headquarters are in Kampsville, across the Illinois River, near the dig that caused the vicinity to be relabeled Koster.

Grafton begins one of the most scenic stretches of the Great River Trail, running south on State Highway 100 past the village of Elsah and on to Alton. Nestled against a bluff, Elsah derives its name and presence from a hamlet in Scotland, with its decorated bridges and stone cottages. Principia College overlooks the town. Pere Marquette State Park, 5,180 acres just north of Grafton, contains many historic intrigues, including the spot where Marquette and Joliet entered Illinois in 1673. There is also evidence of prehistoric Indian life. Dinosaur fossils have been found in the area. A nature museum is located on a 2,000-acre conservation area.

Just outside Grafton is a free river ferry that crosses the Illinois River, just north of the confluence of the Illinois River with the Mississippi, into Calhoun County, a peninsula surrounded on the east and west by rivers. Calhoun County is perhaps the state's most rustic and is the only one without a railroad.

The American Bottom Country

Early production of bountiful crops earned the name of American Bottom for the broad swath of fertile plain reaching along the Mississippi River from Chester north, almost to Alton in southwestern Illinois. In this region the French influence of early exploration and settlement survives.

Just north of Chester lies Fort Kaskaskia State Park, 236 acres of park, reminiscent of the state's earliest history. The French constructed a wooden stockade along the river banks in 1736, rebuilt it in 1761, and destroyed it six years later to prevent British occupation. The park also features the old French home of Pierre Menard, who later became the state's first lieutenant governor.

In the late 19th century, the Mississippi River changed its course, eventually engulfing the original site of Kaskaskia and forming Kaskaskia Island. A small nob of land on the western side of the Mississippi, Kaskaskia Island can only be reached by car by crossing into Missouri at Chester and winding on side roads past St. Mary's and back into Illinois.

The state's first capitol building was located in Kaskaskia, but was moved to Vandalia in 1820. The original capitol building is gone, washed under by the Mississippi 20 years later.

Settled in 1803 by Jesuit priests, Kaskaskia and Cahokia became the chief centers of French life in the area. The island's history boasts of the only other liberty bell in America. Cast 11 years before Philadelphia's bell, the 650-pound bell was cast in France in 1741 and given by Louis XV to his colonists in Illinois for their courage. Technically, Kaskaskia came under British rule by the peace treaty that ended the French and Indian War. Story has it that George Rogers Clark rang the bell to mark the end of his successful journey through Illinois, when he seized the town on July 4, 1778. Clark's expedition led to the inclusion of Illinois in the Louisiana Purchase, obtained from the French by the United States.

French customs are still observed on New Year's Eve in the old French village of Prairie du Rocher, north along State Highway 155. The town's original site was below the river bluff on which Fort de Chartres was built, the strongest of the French forts along the Mississippi. The fort was the site of the French surrender in 1767 when 100 Highlanders of the Black Watch Regiment marched there. The British felt the fort would soon fall into the river and they wisely abandoned it in 1772. The partially restored fort is in a 19-acre state park where, every June, Voyageur Days recall the early days of Indian and French trading along the river.

Cahokia is the next community of distinction along State Highway 3, the Great River Trail in southern Illinois, from East St. Louis south to Cairo. Founded in 1699 as a Seminary of Foreign Missions by the French, Cahokia grew as a fur-trading post into Illinois' first permanent town. Cahokia Courthouse, built in 1737, is distinguished as the oldest building in the state and west of the Alleghenies. It was the site of the first court sessions and elections in Illinois. The courthouse is one of the few surviving examples of French pioneer log architecture. In Cahokia, Ottawa Indian Chief Pontiac, the leading spirit of the French and Indian War, was slain by an Illinois Indian in 1769. The chief's death was avenged by the besiegement and eventual starvation of the Illinois Indians who took refuge on a sandstone monolith located in what is now known as Starved Rock State Park in LaSalle County.

Illinois contains some of the more prominent mounds and excavations of prehistoric Indian Mound Dwellers. The highly developed agricultural society resided in the Mississippi River Valley area of Illinois. More than 10,000 burial and temple mounds remain, some of the more important concentrated at Cahokia Mounds State Park. The largest is Monks Mound, near East St. Louis, standing 20 feet high in places and extending $3\frac{1}{2}$ miles, enclosed in 100 acres. This colossal mound derived its name from the event when Nicolas Jarrot saw no value in the primitive Indian earthworks and gave the land to an order of Trappist Monks, who built a sanctuary at the foot of the largest mound.

The Missouri River joins the Mississippi River beyond the industrial complex of East St. Louis and Granite City. To the west of Wood River, a marker denotes the way down a levee road to the riverbank where Lewis and Clark, on May 14, 1804, launched their journey into the unknown Pacific Northwest.

In the preliminary exploration of Illinois, Joliet and Marquette cut through Indian lands, through bluffs and shoreline brush, to what is now

Alton. Here they were surprised by an awesome rockpainting, the Piasa Bird: today a representation of the Indian painting marks the weathered rock bluff. Alton recalls the misery of the Civil War as the site of a major cemetery for 1,634 Confederate soldiers, who died in a scurvy-ridden prisoner-of-war camp. A 17-foot figure of Victory, set atop a 93-foot-high granite shaft, in Alton City Cemetery, pays tribute to abolitionist editor Elija Lovejoy, who died in 1837 while protecting his press from a pro-slavery mob.

Little Egypt

Southern Illinois breaks into gentle hills, differing greatly from the smooth, vast plain to the north. With the forested foothills of the Ozark Mountains and the fertile river valleys teeming with game, southern Illinois seemed like the Biblical land of Canaan to early settlers, who called it Little Egypt. They first settled in this area, attracted by its easy climate and terrain.

The identity of Little Egypt goes beyond a supposed similarity to the geography of the Nile River Valley in Egypt. It is a state of mind and a way of life, carefully nourished by residents who see their region as an area set apart from the rest of the state. Egypt seems more a part of the Old South than it does of the prosperous Midwest. Except along the river bottoms and in a few other scattered areas, the land is less productive than the north — what is tilled requires much fertilization — and life is economically poorer.

Deep scars from coal-strip mining desecrate some of the land. Mining once promised a grand future and gave the region a dark, bloody history during the first quarter of the 20th century, which rivals the violence of the Old West. Vast coal deposits remain underground. Perry County contains the most productive of Illinois' 55 active coal mines.

Just as Chicago dominates the rest of Illinois, Cairo reigns over Little Egypt. Pronounced "Kay-ro," Illinois' southernmost town at the junction of the Mississippi and Ohio rivers epitomizes the past elegance enjoyed by this land. The 19th-century Victorian-style Magnolia Manor, built by merchant Charles Galighen, bespeaks of a time when the general trend indicated Cairo would surpass Chicago as the industrial center. Old towns, with imposing residences along the Ohio and Mississippi, recall the prosperity the waterways generated before railroads replaced the waters' importance in transporation and commerce.

Cairo enjoyed its peak as a base of Union operations during the Civil War at Fort Defiance, commanded by General Ulysses S. Grant. The rich black delta surrounding Cairo is flooded each spring in areas beyond the protecting dikes. The peninsular shaped Alexander County contains the lowest elevation in the state at Alexander City, along the Mississippi River, only 270 feet above sea level.

Deep South swamps and bald cypress trees of Horseshoe Lake Conservation Area, near Miller City, create some of the most unusual scenery in Illinois. The park bursts into full color from spring to summer when the red buckeye and lotus bloom.

Metropolis, made famous by the comic book super-hero, Superman, is the first major community west of Cairo on the Ohio River. Residents put in a superhuman effort to keep alive the Superman story.

Military and colonial life of the 1700s is re-enacted in an annual festival at Fort Massac, just east of Metropolis. Explorer Clark used Fort Massac to escape from the Indians on his journey to Kaskaskia to claim the Illinois Territory for the United States. His journey took him north through the Ozark Hills, through the wooded gorges, and under rock overhangs at the present Ferne Clyffe State Park, past Goreville, near the Lake of Egypt.

The town of Cypress, farther north, and surrounding Heron Pond, Wildcat Bluff Nature Preserve and Little Black Slough, would seem more appropriate located in Florida than in the Midwest. A more dramatic departure from the prairie seems impossible. Unusual plant life, such as white and chinquapin oak, swamps of cypress and typelo, and creatures such as blue heron, thrive amid sandstone bluffs.

North, via U.S. Highway 45, Vienna begins the Trail of Tears to Jonesboro, commemorating the tragic crossing of 15,000 Cherokee Indians through Illinois, on to North Carolina, and into Oklahoma in the winter of 1838-39. Ice floes made the Mississippi River impassable, forcing the refugees to camp at what is now Trail of Tears State Park north of Jonesboro. Many died during the harsh season. Anna, along the trail on Route 146, is home of the Coon Chase and Goose Calling Festival which, early in October, attracts coonhound fanciers and hunters.

A panoramic view of the Shawnee National Forest is available atop Bald Knob Cross in Trail of Tears State Park. Shawnee National Forest extends over much of lower Little Egypt into nine counties, from the Mississippi River eastward to the Ohio. The region, set in the Little Ozark Mountains — often called the Shawnee Hills — contrasts colorfully with the prairie. Ribbons of mineral deposits paint the country's only east-west range.

Some of the more peculiar rock formations are found at Giant City State Park, 12 miles southeast of Carbondale. The park was so named because of the huge, toppled, cubical stones resembling a city in ruins.

Caves along Bay Creek once protected Indian hunting parties. Down-stream, winds have sculptured a 125-foot-high stone-arch bridge.

A network of lakes — Crab Orchard, Little Grassy, and Devil's Kitchen — and marshlands provides a winter roost for Canadian geese in Williamson County. Belle Smith Springs links the eastern part of the Shawnee Forest with the more extensive western portion. North, near Delwood, splashes Burden Falls, one of the state's more popular cascades.

East of Eddyville, river birch and red maples fringe the sheer cliffs of Lusk Creek Canyon, where clubmoss, an Ice Age plant, can be found.

Golconda is the center of outdoor activity in Pope County and hosts the county deer festival. The celebration kicks off the hunting season with three days of parades, pageants, food, and spirits. Founded by Revolutionary War hero James Lusk, Golconda marks the spot where the Cherokee Indians entered Illinois.

Cave-in-Rock, where the Ohio River bends north toward Indiana, has a 108-foot deep canyon that served as a sacred region for the Indians;

as a hideout for notorious pirates of the 1700s, such as Sam Mason; and for outlaws of the 1800s, such as the Harper brothers, who preyed upon the river's flatboat traffic.

Karbers Ridge leads the way northwest to the Garden of the Gods. Over the past 200-million years, nature's elements have created a remarkable scattering of sandstone formations in the rugged, bristling foothills. Some of the more spectacular outcroppings are Fat Man's Squeeze, Anvil Rock, Tower of Babel, Camel Rock, and Buzzard Roost. Sheer walls form a natural fortress, which, according to legend, Indians used to trap buffalo. The serpentine path of Rim Rock Trail climbs up an ancient stone wall, now in ruins.

The prairie farmland is patched with towns: DuQuoin, home of the nation's richest harness race, the Hambletonian; Mt. Vernon, the southernmost top on Lincoln's circuit; Salem, where oil wells gushed in the boom of the 1930s; and Vandalia, the state's capital for 20 years. Here, our wanderings through the great prairie state of Illinois come to an end.